BERKLEE PRESS

DRUM STUDIES:

CONCEPTS, READING, PHRASING, AND TECHNIQUE

DAVE VOSE

Edited by Jonathan Feist

Berklee Press

Vice President: David Kusek
Dean of Continuing Education: Debbie Cavalier
Chief Operating Officer: Robert F. Green
Managing Editor: Jonathan Feist
Editorial Assistants: Andrea Penzel, Jacqueline Sim
Cover Designer: Kathy Kikkert
Cover Photo: Shane Corcoran Photography LLC

ISBN 978-0-87639-117-4

1140 Boylston Street
Boston, MA 02215-3693 USA
(617) 747-2146

Visit Berklee Press Online at
www.berkleepress.com

DISTRIBUTED BY

HAL•LEONARD®
CORPORATION
7777 W. BLUEMOUND RD. P.O. BOX 13819
MILWAUKEE, WISCONSIN 53213

Visit Hal Leonard Online at
www.halleonard.com

CONTENTS

ACKNOWLEDGMENTS

My thanks go to everyone at Berklee Press, especially Jonathan Feist. I also would like to acknowledge influential percussion teachers who I have studied with, including Fred Buda, Gerry Shellmer, Alfsons Grieder, Gary Burton, and the late Alan Dawson. I also studied with the following on arranging and composition techniques, including Paul Schmeling, Bob Freedman, Ted Pease, and the late Hugo Norden. I would like to thank photographer Shane Corcoran of York, Maine. Finally, as a member of the Berklee faculty, I have the magnificent opportunity to collaborate with fellow faculty and students. Both groups are engaging, informative, and inspiring. I am truly blessed for many reasons.

INTRODUCTION

Drummers often use orchesral and rudimental snare drum books to develop their reading and technical skills. While these are helpful, most have little resemblance to the rhythms and phrasings actually played by drum set players. *Drum Studies* combines what's best in both common types of books, and also includes many concepts commonly used by drum set players.

You may be wondering about the differences between the standard types of approach. The typical orchestral book will have a variety of rhythms in several meters but rarely with syncopated rhythms, which are common in contemporary drum set performance. With rudimental snare drum books, some are traditional, mostly in 2/4 and 6/8. The more contemporary rudimental books have more variety. Rudimental books will present stickings and include various technical and rudimental challenges.

A competent drum set performer will have reading skills, technique to execute a variety of patterns, and the ability to play in a manner that conveys appropriate taste and musicality. These can be achieved by practicing material that has a variety of rhythms and notational appearances, technical challenges, and contemporary phrase structures and concepts. *Drum Studies* includes exercises to help you improve all these components.

This Book Is for You

Drum Studies includes material that is practical and challenging, and organized in a manner to encourage development. Whatever your style of drumming, these patterns and techniques will help you develop the necessary skills to become a better player.

In This Book

Drum Studies includes fifty musical drum pieces, each of which concentrates on four important aspects of performance: concepts, reading, phrasing, and technique. Some chapters have the snare drum notated only, while others also include the bass drum and hi-hat parts. A variety of notational appearances is included to expose you to more reading challenges. The stickings provided here are not necessarily the most typical. Instead, when stickings are indicated, they are to introduce a variety of sounds to the notated patterns, as well as to aid in the development of the performer's technical proficiency.

How to Get the Most out of This Book

To get the most out of this book, you need to understand how it is set up. The pieces have been designed to be challenging, enjoyable, and most important of all, musical. For a musician to be musical, one should always be aware of fundamentals such as tone, dynamics, articulations, phrasing, and the overall purpose of the piece.

Each piece is introduced with a short description of the concept behind the piece, and any special factors about reading, phrasing, and finally, the technique being used. Read these introductions first, while you look over the music. Hopefully, you will have an excellent teacher that can lead you through the pieces and provide input. If you do not, you will need some fundamental knowledge of reading drum notation. High-level beginners and intermediate-level drummers will find this book particularly useful. If you need a more basic book to develop your reading skills, check out my book entitled, *The Reading Drummer*, also published by Berklee Press.

CHAPTER 1

Set the Tone

CONCEPTS: Chapter 1 includes eighth-note syncopation, dynamics, and accents. Observing these markings will help make your performance expressive.

READING: In this chaper, you will find dotted quarter notes, quarter notes, eighth notes, and sixteenth notes. The four sixteenth-note grouping will always resolve to the downbeat.

PHRASING: "Set the Tone" is written in 8-bar phrases, which is the most common phrase length in music.

TECHNIQUE: Practice the piece at a variety of tempos, as indicated at the beginning. Be aware of the drum tone when performing dynamics and articulations.
Try recording your performance to analyze your quality.

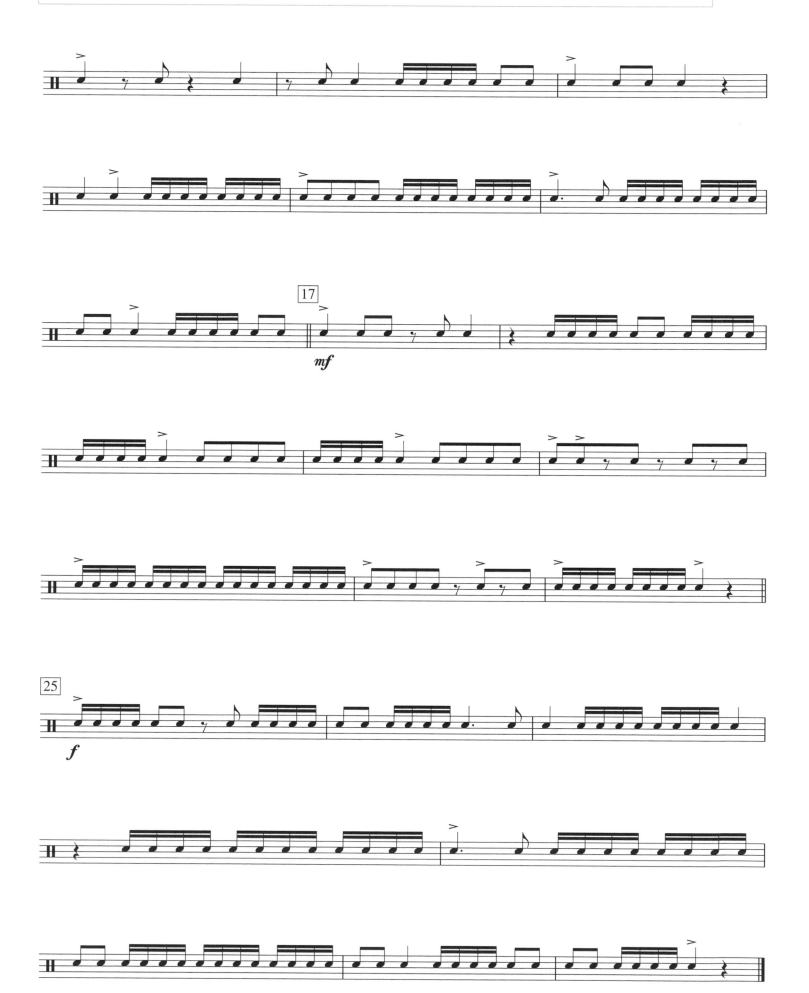

CHAPTER 2

Dedication

CONCEPT: The *crescendo* and the *decrescendo* are used to create intensity and suspense.

READING: "Dedication" includes the eighth and two sixteenth-note pattern (♪♫, also notated as ♫♫).

PHRASING: 8-bar phrases. Observe how the eighth bar transitions into the next phrase.

TECHNIQUE: Maintain sound quality during the dynamic changes. Also, be careful not to rush or slow down when performing a crescendo or decrescendo.

CHAPTER 3

Three Times Is a Charm

CONCEPT: The 3/4 meter and stickings are introduced. Stickings add their own articulated sound and an expressive quality to the performance.

READING: "Three Times Is a Charm" introduces the 3/4 meter. Also, you will again experience the eighth and two sixteenths pattern (♪♫). In addition, you will have the notation of the two sixteenths and an eighth pattern (♫♪), also notated as three sixteenths and a sixteenth rest (♫♪↗). The tie (⌣) indicates that the tone is to be sustained for the combined duration. The sustain will be accomplished if there is a roll or if the instrument that is struck rings. When striking a drum that does not ring, only play the attack.

PHRASING: 8-bar phrases are common in music. "Three Times Is a Charm" is composed with 8-bar phrases throughout.

TECHNIQUE: Control the accuracy of the rhythm when applying the stickings. The stickings indicated are not necessarily the most typical. Instead, they are written to add variety and to encourage technical development.

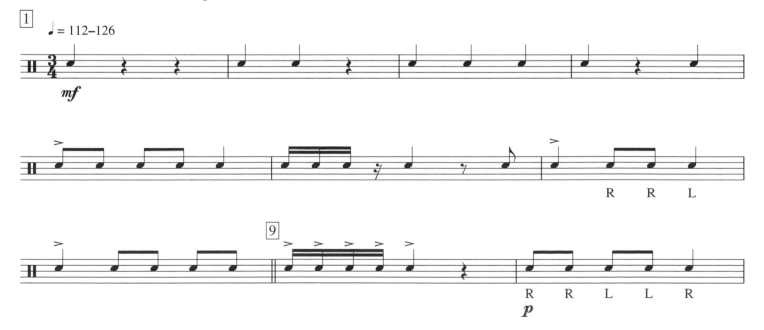

CHAPTER 4

Two for the Price of One

CONCEPTS: This piece has 8-bar phrases with flowing rhythmic patterns in 2/4 meter.

READING: Continue to count when performing in 2/4 meter. Also, you will experience the four sixteenth-note pattern unresolved. Additionally, notice that the rhythms are notated on a single line staff.

PHRASING: Again, this piece uses 8-bar phrases. Notice that in some of the eighth measures (8, 16, 32, 56, 64), the rhythm resolves to the down-beat, while in others (24, 40, 48), the rhythm leads you into the next phrase.

TECHNIQUE: Single paradiddles occur in bar 20. Perform this exercise with a variety of tempos. Playing steady quarter notes on the bass drum will help the development of your coordination.

CHAPTER 5

Transitions Count

CONCEPTS: You will find that the use of sixteenth-note *syncopation* is common in many contemporary styles. Syncopation is when the offbeat note is emphasized. It often occurs two or more times in succession. Syncopation adds an element of suspense, as the listener wonders when the syncopation will resolve.

READING: In this lesson, find the sixteenth-eighth-sixteenth pattern (♫) and the sixteenth rest and three sixteenth-note pattern (♫). Also notice the *pickup* note. Pickup note(s) occur before the beginning of the piece and are very common, as they lead to a strong note on beat 1.

PHRASING: Notice when the sixteenth-note syncopated patterns resolve. Also, be aware of how the crescendo is used as the transition into measure 17.

TECHNIQUE: Be careful of accuracy when performing the sixteenth-note syncopated rhythms. Relate the placement of the syncopated notes to where they are performed within the full sixteenth-note grouping.

CHAPTER 6

High and Low

CONCEPT: "High and Low" uses the snare drum and bass drum in combination. Included here, find dynamics and the opportunity to express musicality.

READING: The challenge is in reading two instrumental parts simultaneously.

PHRASING: At bar 9, there is a one-bar *ostinato* that is "waltz-like." The 4-bar phrase at bar 9 has a form of AAAB, which means that bars 9, 10, and 11 are all the same and bar 12 is different. The next 4-bar phrase is structured as ABAC.

In bars 25 to 27, there is a rhythm played on the snare drum that is a 3-beat pattern superimposed over the 4/4 meter, while at the same time, the bass drum plays on beats 2 and 4.

TECHNIQUE: Be aware that the two parts (snare drum and bass drum) relate to each other to create a cumulative effect. Make the foot parts an extension of the hand parts to create total musical flow.

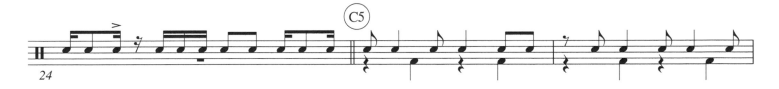

CHAPTER 7

Come on Down

CONCEPT: "Come on Down" is in 2/4 meter. You will find more sixteenth-note groupings and flams.

READING: When reading in 2/4 meter, count the downbeats as "one, two."

Notice the use of two sixteenth-note groupings at A4 , A7 , B3 , as well as other locations.

PHRASING: This piece has all 8-bar phrases. Observe the rhythms in the last bar of each phrase. Notice that at times (bar 8), the rhythm resolves on the downbeat. This creates a feeling of starting the next phrase fresh, as opposed to the rhythm moving into the next phrase (bar 16), which creates motion.

TECHNIQUE: Develop a sticking formula that feels comfortable when playing the sixteenth-note rhythms. A common sticking is playing the first and third note of the 4-note grouping with the right hand, and the second and fourth note with the left hand. See below.

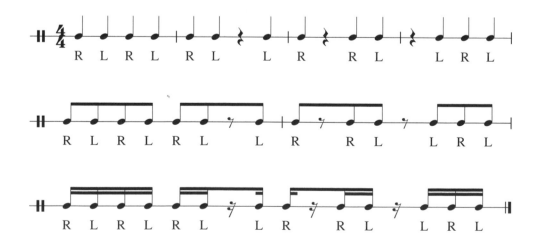

Flams are used in this piece. Generally, when playing flams, the grace note should be struck softer than the primary note. To execute this, strike the grace note from a lower stick height.

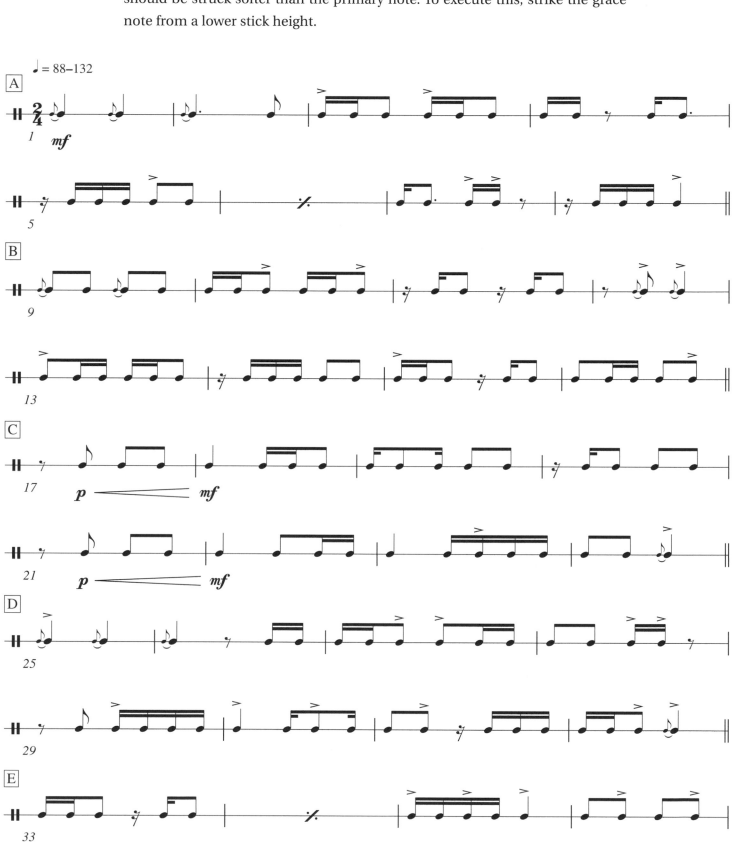

CHAPTER 8

Roll with It

CONCEPT: This lesson includes the double-stroke roll, which is a commonly used method to sustain a sound. Also, notice the use of the eighth-note triplet.

READING: Having three slashes above or below a note is a common method of notating a roll. If the note has a beam on it, an additional two slashes are used to indicate the roll.

The *eighth-note triplet* (𝄾) is a common grouping in which we perform three eighth notes in the time span of two eighth notes. The notes should be evenly spaced. Using "3" above or below the grouping is essential to indicate that it is a triplet.

Finally, notice that the stems are pointing down. Stems down is an option that is often used in snare drum notation regardless of the time signature.

PHRASING: In "Roll with It," the second phrase is four measures long, and the rest are all eight measures. Notice that the fourth phrase uses an effect that is called a *rhythmic accelerando*, meaning that the tempo does not change but the rhythm simulates an accelerando.

TECHNIQUE: The double-stroke roll requires special attention. The individual notes of a double-stroke roll should be clearly articulated. Practice the roll separately before applying it to this piece.

A range of tempos is suggested. However, the number of notes played within the roll durations may need to be altered. For example, the number of strokes to fill the value of duration at a tempo of 120 beats per minute is different then what will be needed when the tempo is 80 beats per minute.

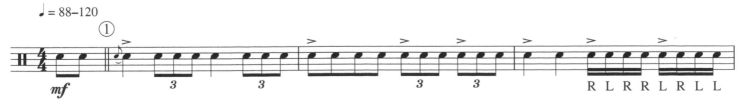

CHAPTER 9

Another Thought

CONCEPT: This piece displays reading in *6/8* and *12/8* time signatures. Also, you will experience the *orchestral buzz roll*. In orchestral music, all rolls are notated with three slashes accompanying the note (♪). However, when a composer wishes to distinguish between buzz rolls and double-stroke rolls, buzz rolls are notated with the Z marking over the note (♪), while double-stroke rolls use the slash notation.

READING: The 6/8 time signature has six beats per measure with the eighth note getting one beat. The 6/8 meter provides a feeling of "two," as the pulsation is on the first and fourth eighth note. Therefore, when performing "Another Thought," tap the bass drum on beats 1 and 4. When performing in 6/8, use a preliminary count off of "one, two, one, two," which represents beats 1 and 4.

"Another Thought" flows into 12/8 at B1. This meter has four pulses occurring on beats 1, 4, 7, and 10. Tap the bass drum on those pulses.

PHRASING: Notice at measure 9 that the phrase starting here is seven measures long. A24 is a 3-bar phrase that transitions into B1.

TECHNIQUE: Orchestral buzz rolls are performed by pressing the sticks into the drumhead and allowing the sticks to bounce multiple times. Feel the response, and work with it to get a smooth buzz sound.

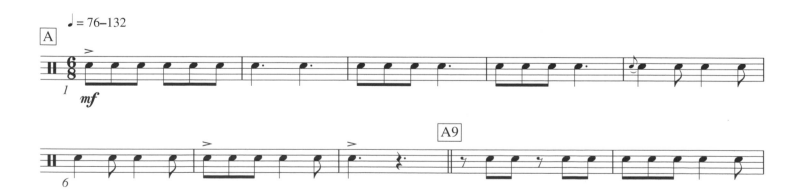

CHAPTER 10

Express It!

CONCEPT: "Express It!" includes several reading situations including note abbreviations and more of the eighth-note triplet grouping. Also, you will find more use of the double-stroke roll and the buzz roll.

READING: In "Express It!" you will encounter note abbreviations. Occasionally in percussion music, you will see these, as the writer may find these to be more economical without musical sacrifice.

Below, find a chart of note abbreviations.

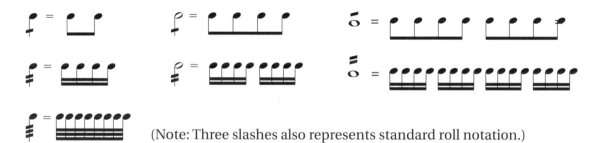

(Note: Three slashes also represents standard roll notation.)

Starting in bar 14, you will see beaming over the bar line. Generally, beams are used to display beat divisions. These beams are to show a pattern working as a unit.

PHRASING: At measure 7, you find a rhythm that is three beats long and repeats. This rhythm sounds like it is in the 3/4 time signature, but here, it is notated over the 4/4 time signature. This effect is not rare in contemporary music, as it can create an interesting expressive quality, especially when other musicians are included. The rhythm recurs in measure 10 in half its value. This is an example of *diminution*.

TECHNIQUE: "Express It!" includes the double-stroke roll, buzz rolls, flams, and stickings. These devices are some of the common technical challenges in drumming.

CHAPTER 11

Brush It Up!

CONCEPT: "Brush It Up!" is written for the use of brushes. Brushes in drumming have a long history, especially in jazz. Brushes provide a very different sound and striking technique, as compared to drumsticks.

READING: The entire piece is to be read with a swing interpretation (♫=♪♪). Sixteenth notes should be played with straight interpretation and are meant to "go against the grain," to provide contrast.

PHRASING: Measure 17 is a 4-measure phrase that is meant to transition into a mood change. At measure 21, we have a 6-bar phrase.

TECHNIQUE: When the note has roll slashes, perform a single stroke roll. Otherwise, perform sweeps across the drumhead to sustain the note durations. When you encounter a staccato marking, simply tap the note. Also, play the bass drum on all four downbeats and the hi-hat on beats 2 and 4.

CHAPTER 12

Real World Experience

CONCEPT: This piece has the bass drum notated and a large variety of sixteenth-note rhythms. You will also find the three-stroke ruff.

READING: Two patterns are introduced: the first and fourth notes of the four sixteenth-note pattern (♪♪) and a dotted eighth beamed to a sixteenth (♪. ♪).

At various locations you will find the three-stroke ruff. As with the single grace note, the double grace notes receive no official value in the measure.

PHRASING: At A9 , we have a 3-measure phrase leading you into a 4-measure phrase in 4/4, then back to 3/4.

"Real World Experience" ends with a 7-measure phrase.

TECHNIQUE: The 3-stroke ruff is performed by using rebound, but unlike the buzz roll, the notes need to be controlled so that only two notes are played. They should be clearly articulated.

CHAPTER 13

Connecting the Dots

CONCEPT: "Connecting the Dots" explores sound sources including striking on the rim and the removal of the snares.

READING: This lesson includes performing a variety of common sixteenth-note patterns and reading to create a variety of sounds.

PHRASING: Bars 19 and 20 utilize a pattern that spans over five beats while notated in 4/4 meter. Also, three measures from the end, there is a buzz roll with a *fermata*. Following the fermata is a *caesura*, which means to cut off the sound. The pause will create a dramatic effect.

Finally, play the conclusion at a *presto* tempo for a final explosive and exciting ending.

TECHNIQUE: In measures A5 and C11 , play a "stick on stick" rim shot. Perform these rim shots to create a tone quality of the pitch going from low to high. This can be achieved by applying pressure on the drumhead with the stick as you strike it. Also, look ahead to prepare for your movement to the rim, so that it will be executed smoothly. Be sure to find a location on the drumsticks that provides the best tone when striking the rim.

At bar A6 , the grace note of the flam should be buzzed.

CHAPTER 14

A Walk in the Park

CONCEPT: "A Walk in the Park" is orchestrated for the snare drum, bass drum, and hi-hat cymbals.

READING: Just like "A Walk in the Park," hearing the sounds of a snare drum, bass, and hi-hat cymbals will be music to your ears. With that said, reading for these three voices might be new for you. Look ahead as you are reading to allow your limbs to respond instinctively to the music.

An abrupt tempo change takes place at measure 21. Learn the tempos separately, and memorize them. It is not unusual to make immediate tempo changes in music.

PHRASING: The 3/4 section starting at measure 9 is twelve measures long.

The 3-beat phrase starting at measure 33 continues nine times, but starting at measure 37, the time signature changes to 4/4.

TECHNIQUE: When you have long durations notated for the hi-hat cymbals, allow them to ring. Close them when the duration is complete.

At measures 21 to 24, the crescendos are meant for the hand parts only. Keep the bass drum and hi-hat parts consistent in volume.

Let Ring

CHAPTER 15

Logical Illusions

CONCEPT: The mood of the 12/8 meter and 9/8 meter, with wide dynamic and tempo changes, should make "Logical Illusions" an interesting piece to perform.

READING: The 12/8 meter should be played with four pulses per measure.

[C3] has *quadruplets*. These should be performed by spacing four notes evenly within each pulse.

The 9/8 meter should be played with three even pulses per measure.

PHRASING: The final section makes use of stickings to provide a variety of phraseology as you approach the conclusion.

TECHNIQUE: Be careful of tempo control when performing the accelerando at measures 26 to 28.

When performing the fast tempo that begins at [D], give the accents a quick accented snap followed by a quick stick return to be able to perform the *mezzo-forte* dynamic level.

The stickings will add some challenges. Practice them slowly at first.

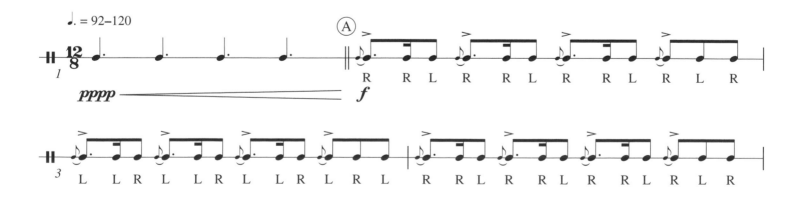

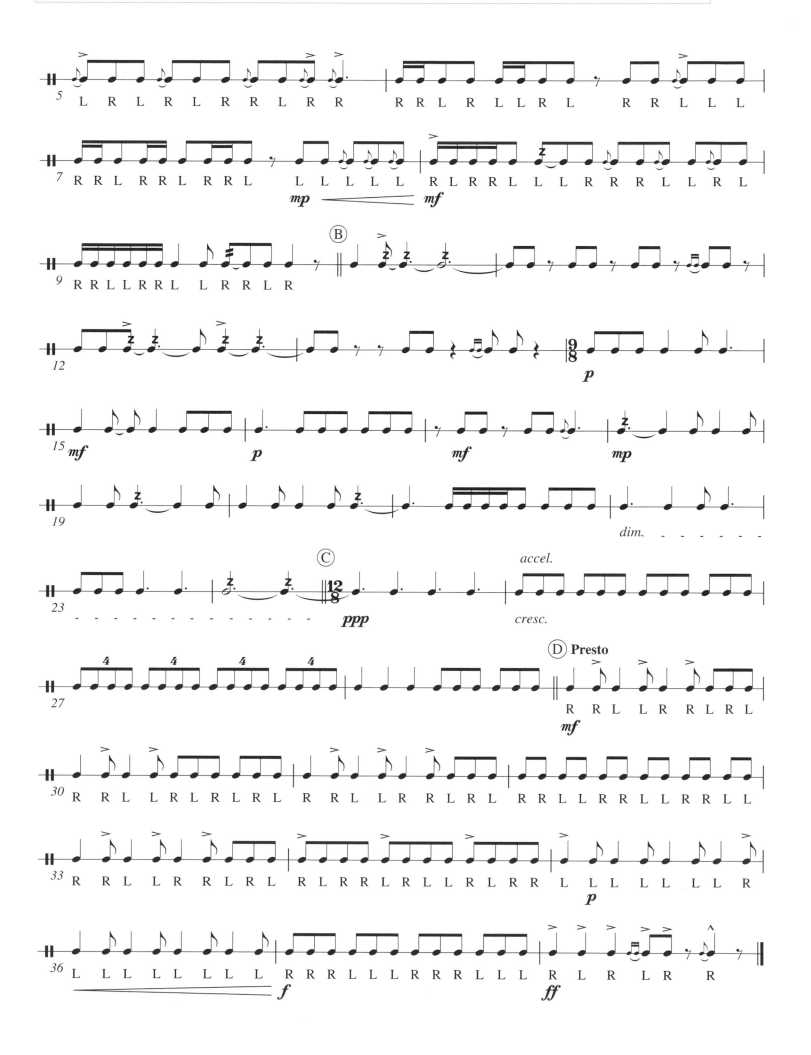

CHAPTER 16

Double It Up

CONCEPT: "Double It Up" makes use of the concept of double time and half time. Measures 1 to 20 have you start performing at 120 beats per minute and then cutting that in half to 60 beats per minute. After a *grand pause* on the fourth beat of measure 20, the piece picks up the tempo ($\quarternote$ = 144) with an emphasis on eighth-note syncopation and stickings.

READING: Observe the tempo markings indicated above the staff. Measure 21 starts with extensive use of eighth-note syncopation. This is characterized by frequent use of quarter notes on the upbeats and ties over the bar line and over the imaginary bar line.

PHRASING: The first twenty bars function as a complete statement. A listener of your performance will be intrigued by the back-and-forth tempo changes.

Measure 21 begins a new statement following a grand pause with extensive eighth-note syncopation, which provides a spirit of forward momentum.

TECHNIQUE: The number of hand motions used when executing a roll depends on the tempo. Generally, when performing a roll, the sound is of a sustained buzz or rapid double strokes. If there is no indication of the number of strokes to be performed, which is most commonly the situation, you should fill the sound by playing as many notes as possible without the result sounding forced. The stickings from Ⓒ to the end deserve special attention.

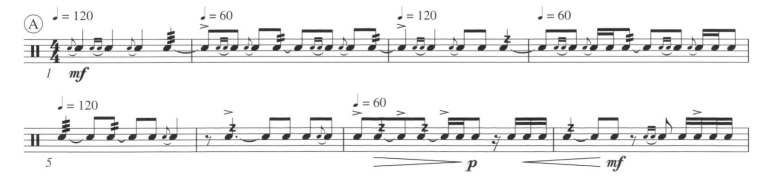

CHAPTER 17

Connect to It

CONCEPT: This piece should have a smooth flow to it with an occasional *maestoso* interpretation when performing the reoccurring rhythm that occurs in the first two measures. In contrast, there are some sixteenth patterns (bars 9–10) that resemble a "groove" interpretation.

READING: The notes are written on a single line staff with the noteheads on the line.

   Also, notice the use of note abbreviations and an extended buzz roll with accents.

PHRASING: As always, be aware of phrase lengths. The first phrase is six measures long. At rehearsal number 7, the phrase is nine measures long.

   A 3/4 bar is used to enter the extended buzz rolls, which creates a feeling of anticipation and energy.

TECHNIQUE: Bars 16 to 18 have several decrescendos, which need careful observation to achieve the correct levels.

   Bar 25 begins an extended buzz roll with accents. The accents should be forced buzzes and not single notes.

   At bar 35, you need to make an abrupt technique change to execute the open double-stroke roll, after playing many buzz rolls.

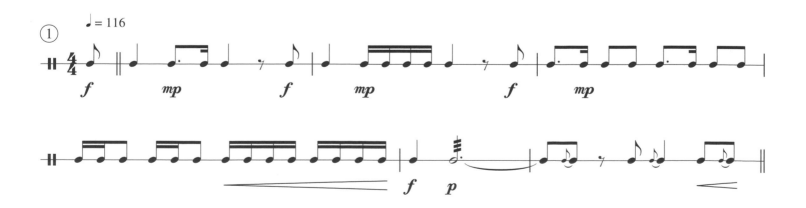

CHAPTER 18

Four on the Floor

CONCEPT: "Four on the Floor" is written to be played on a floor tom. After the note is struck and the tone of the note rings for its full value, apply hand muffling to cut the duration.

READING: A large variety of common rhythms are used here, but you must be very aware of the duration of the note, and you must not let the dampening of the notes impede your performance. The plus symbol (+) at measure 17 means to muffle the drum with one hand as you strike it with the other.

PHRASING: 17 and 22 combine to form an 8-bar transition into 25 .
   At 29 , we have a 6-bar phrase.
   At 35 , we end with a 6-bar phrase.

TECHNIQUE: The close awareness of note durations will add a new type of technique and musicianship to your skills.

CHAPTER 19

Movin' It

CONCEPT: "Movin' It" is to be played at a fast tempo throughout.

READING: Reading at fast tempos requires consistent focus. The smallest distraction can cause an error. Maintain your focus.

PHRASING: Ⓒ starts a section with a swing interpretation. Bars 25 to 27 have a 2-beat phrase notated in 3/4 meter with dynamic changes.

TECHNIQUE: With fast tempos, you need to constantly be looking ahead to be physically and psychologically ready to perform the next passage. Do not have excessive stick movement, as wasted motion can be your worst enemy with fast tempos.

CHAPTER 20

P.T.C.: Play the Composition

CONCEPT: The use of syncopation, articulations, and dynamics within the "two feel" gives this piece its own unique styling.

READING: *Cut time* has two beats to a measure, with the half note getting one beat. Also, you will experience the 3/2 meter.

PHRASING: The rhythms in the first eight bars create a feeling of an accelerando without a tempo change. Also, bars 25 to 31 form a 7-bar phrase.

TECHNIQUE: Measures 5 to 9 make use of the drum rudiment, *flam taps*. Changing roll technique requires special attention. Measure 37 has a double-stroke roll, measure 38 a buzz, and measure 39 a double-stroke roll again.

CHAPTER 21

Dig Deeper

CONCEPT: Rhythmic variation, striking on the rim, swing interpretation, and stickings all add up to make this piece very diverse.

READING: Many rhythmic patterns are used here including the four-over-three (4:3) pattern and quarter note triplet with the quarter notes divided. The 4:3 pattern that begins this piece is not as difficult as at first you might think. It is the exact same rhythm as this:

The swing eighths at B should have a triplet interpretation.

PHRASING: Double stickings within a triplet passage always create an interesting phrasing effect.

The swing section starting at B is 15 bars long.

TECHNIQUE: At A3, use a one-handed, left-handed buzz. At C3, notice that the grace notes on the quarter-note triplets are buzzed.

Stickings are challenging here, especially at C5 where drummers do not often use stickings in this manner. These are called "inside-out diddles."

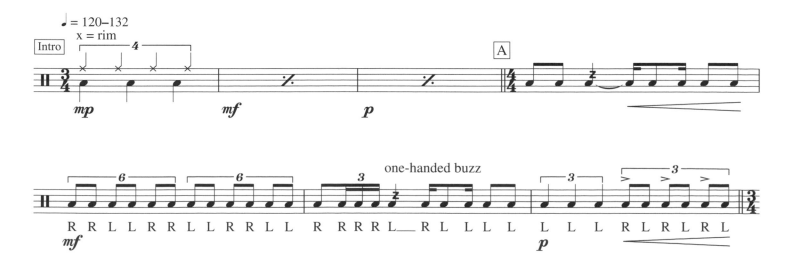

CHAPTER 22

Bridge the Gap

CONCEPT: You will find a large variety of mixed subdivisions with dynamics in this piece.

READING: In this piece, the sixteenth notes with the slash through the stem will result in the notes being played as two 32nd notes. In the triplet grouping, the slashes will result in the eighth note of the triplet becoming two 16th-note triplets.

PHRASING: The first section has repeat marks. The first time, play it *mp*. Then on the second playing, perform it *mf*.

At bar 26, there is a 4-bar rhythmic phrase that will simulate an accelerando. The tempo should not fluctuate.

TECHNIQUE: It is challenging going from triplet rolls to 32nd-note rolls (measures 12 to 14). Listen carefully for the quality of sound and proper note spacing.

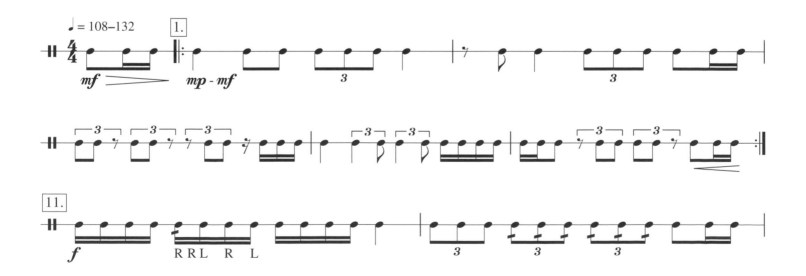

CHAPTER 23

Exploring the Region

CONCEPT: In "Exploring the Regions," you will become more aware of the tones that your drum can produce. The custom staff will display for you where to strike the drumhead. Notice the tone differences.

READING: Occasionally, a percussionist is called upon to read on a custom staff. When reading on this staff, you should strike at the edge of the drum when reading notes on the top line, strike between the edge and the middle when reading the middle line, and strike at the center of the drum when reading the bottom line.

PHRASING: This piece starts with an 8-bar intro. The piece then moves into a 5-bar phrase that repeats. From there, "Exploring the Region" does just that, as you will find syncopated rhythms notated to be played on the three different striking zones.

TECHNIQUE: Look ahead to prepare yourself for the moves to the three striking zones.

Your buzz-roll striking technique may need to be altered when striking in the different areas. When the tone is more dry, you may need to provide more strokes than when the snares are resonating more frequently.

TOP LINE: Edge (near rim)
MIDDLE LINE: Between center and edge
BOTTOM LINE: Center

CHAPTER 24

Environment of the Drum

CONCEPT: This piece includes more rhythms with flowing sixteenth-note rhythmic patterns with mixed subdivisions. These are common occurrences in music, and all drummers need to become very proficient with them.

READING: Included are a variety of sixteenth-note and triplet patterns. Also, notice the use of a displaced eighth-note pattern in bar 28. The eighths are syncopated (sixteenth-note style), and then resolve on the downbeat in bar 29.

PHRASING: Bars 9 and 10 make up a 2-bar interlude.

Syncopated sixteenth notes with a crescendo are used as the phrase linkage into bar 18.

There is a 5-bar phrase at measure 18 and a 6-bar phrase at measure 23.

TECHNIQUE: There are many ways to approach stickings when dealing with sixteenth-note patterns. You should have an approach that you want to work with, by this stage of your development. As you progress, it will also be beneficial to explore a variety of sticking possibilities. Regardless of the approach that you use, strive for a controlled sound when striking with both the right and left stick.

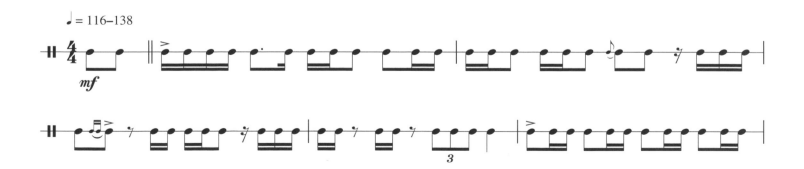

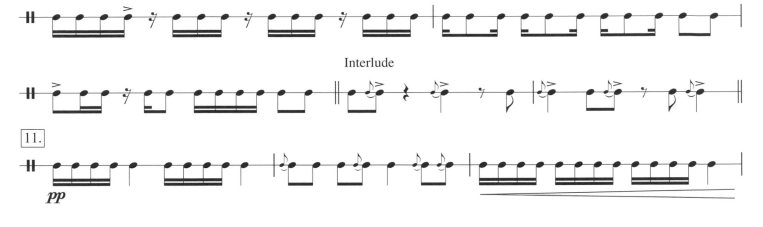

Interlude

CHAPTER 25

Drumscape

CONCEPT: "Drumscape" includes interplay between the snare drum and the bass drum in a variety of time signatures.

READING: The notation in this piece uses a single-line staff for the snare drum and a second single-line staff for the bass drum.

The beaming used in the first bar, and several other measures, is for phrasing purposes. Generally, sixteenth notes are beamed in such a way that each beat is visible and does not overlap a downbeat.

Also, you will find three different time signatures. The pulse is consistent between them.

PHRASING: The beaming that occurs in the first measure and other places is to help display how the group of notes should relate to each other as a unit. Maintain a constant flow when performing the interplay between the bass drum and snare drum.

TECHNIQUE: Observe the sticking patterns. Maintain control when performing the diddles.

When the bass drum and the snare are notated to be struck at the same time, make sure that they hit precisely together.

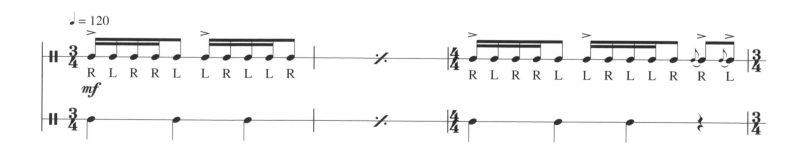

CHAPTER 26

Once Upon a Rhythm

CONCEPT: "Once Upon a Rhythm" begins with rolls into single and triple paradiddles. It jolts into a fast tempo on the third beat of measure 11 and then returns to the first tempo. The piece gets powerful only to finish with a *morendo* (drifting off in the distance).

READING: Observe all the dramatic effects that occur in this piece. This piece is enhanced with stickings, embellishments, and other effects.

PHRASING: Notice the paradiddle stickings during the eighth-note triplets at measure 23. The 4-note sticking pattern notated during the 3-note pattern of the triplets creates an interesting sound quality. The accents of the paradiddles occur at the same location as half-note triplets at measure 25. At 26, double paradiddles are phrased over the bar line.

TECHNIQUE: Notice a staccato buzz roll in measure 16. Execute this staccato buzz roll with both sticks striking at the same time. At measure 19, "strike" both sticks to the drumhead at the same time for the long, accented buzz rolls.

CHAPTER 27

Scatter

CONCEPTS: The emphasis here is on a quick tempo with both interplay and support provided by the bass drum and the hi-hat cymbals.

READING: Three-voice reading takes place with "Scatter." Always look ahead to help the parts flow from one to the other.

There is a short, two-beat accelerando going from measure 31 to 32.

The dynamics at measures 7 to 11 are meant for both the snare and the bass drum.

The dynamics above the staff at measure 38 are for the snare part only.

When going from the 4/4 meter to the 12/8 meter at measures 39 and 40, keep the pulse consistent.

PHRASING: The phrases are displayed with double bar lines. Also, be aware of the inner phrases, noticing how one rhythmic pattern moves to the next.

TECHNIQUE: At bar 20, the sixteenth-note rhythm provides a pseudo-Latin feel. Bring out the accents with the right hand, and keep the left relaxed as it fills between the accents.

CHAPTER 28

All Notes Count

CONCEPT: This piece has mixed meters with an emphasis on 7/8.

READING: In any time signature that has 8 as its denominator, analyze it to determine how the notes are grouped. Groupings are determined by how the notes are beamed and by the note durations. The first 7/8 is grouped as 2 + 2 + 3.

PHRASING: This piece starts with an 11-measure phrase.

Measures 18 to the end pulsate the 7/8 time signature with a 2 + 2 + 3 grouping, with the exception of one measure of 3/4 at bar 41.

TECHNIQUE: There are several technical challenges here. At B, we find a flam passage that turns into staccato buzzed accents. When playing the sixteenth notes with intermixed grace notes, keep the stick height of the grace notes low to the drum. Bar 23 features single and double para- diddles in 7/8.

CHAPTER 29

It's My Inspiration

CONCEPT: In this piece, you will experience complex interplay between the snare drum and bass drum parts. The coordinated rhythmic performance will help develop your coordination.

READING: Many sixteenth-note combinations exist here that are played between the snare drum and bass drum.

PHRASING: Practice to achieve a smooth flow of rhythm between the snare drum and the bass drum. In some cases, the bass drum is creating interplay with the snare drum, while at other times, it provides support and texture to the snare drum part.

The bass drum part from bars 6 to 9 is phrased with a 5-beat pattern while the music is notated in 4/4.

TECHNIQUE: Be precise at coordinating the unison snare and bass drum on the dotted eighth note in bar 2 as well as the last sixteenth note in bar 12.

The piece is performed at *mf* throughout.

Observe your accent quality, as many of the accents occur on syncopated notes.

At times, we have consecutive sixteenth notes placed in the bass drum part. These may take some individual attention to perform accurately and with a consistent sound quality.

CHAPTER 30

Articulate It!

CONCEPT: This piece uses many rhythmic patterns and also a *ritardando*. Always strive for clearly articulated rhythms.

READING: "Articulate It!" includes reading accented sixteenth notes and triplet groupings. The rhythms are notated on a single line staff with the stems pointing down.

PHRASING: Analyze the phrases before you begin.

Going from measure 30 to 31 can be challenging, as you must perform a slow quarter-note triplet and then suddenly go to a quarter-note triplet at a faster tempo.

A crescendo is used to transition into bar 17.

TECHNIQUE: Bar 12 has a short roll on the last note of an eighth-note triplet, going into a quarter-note triplet. Be careful of the timing.

When playing the accents starting at bar 17, it should sound like two players. One player plays steady sixteenth notes while the other player performs accents.

Notice the staccato buzz at measure 23.

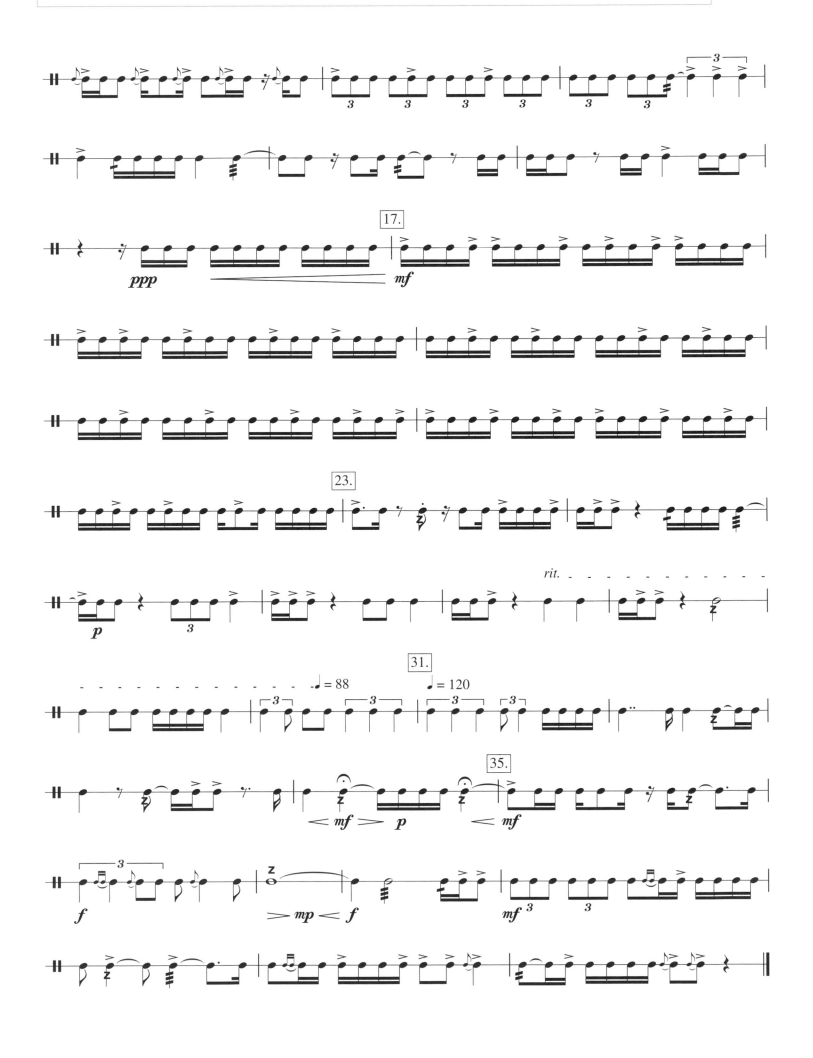

CHAPTER 31

Syncopation Mania

CONCEPT: As the title implies, "Syncopation Mania" is loaded with rhythmic sixteenth-note syncopation. The rhythms used are enhanced with grace notes and rolls.

READING: In this piece, you will become adept at reading syncopated sixteenth rhythms. You will be reading and performing them with roll and grace-note embellishments.

PHRASING: "Syncopation Mania" has all 8-measures phrases. As always, notice how the phrases are linked together.

TECHNIQUE: Try interpreting the double grace notes three different ways:

1. Open (somewhat like 16th-note triplets)
2. Strict (32nd notes)
3. Tight (somewhat like 64th notes)

CHAPTER 32

My Old Friend Rudi

CONCEPT: This piece is rudimental in styling. It is in 2/4 time with flowing patterns. Accents and stickings are a major part of the interpretation of this piece.

READING: At this stage of your development, the rhythms here should not seem too complex. Patterns, stickings, and accents are more of the focus.

PHRASING: All phrases are eight measures long. Notice how some patterns repeat.

TECHNIQUE: When playing notes that occur close together, it is best to play the single grace notes close to the drum. Therefore, control of stick heights becomes essential.

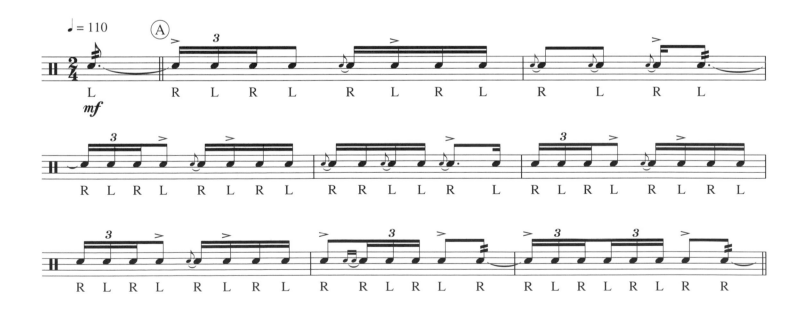

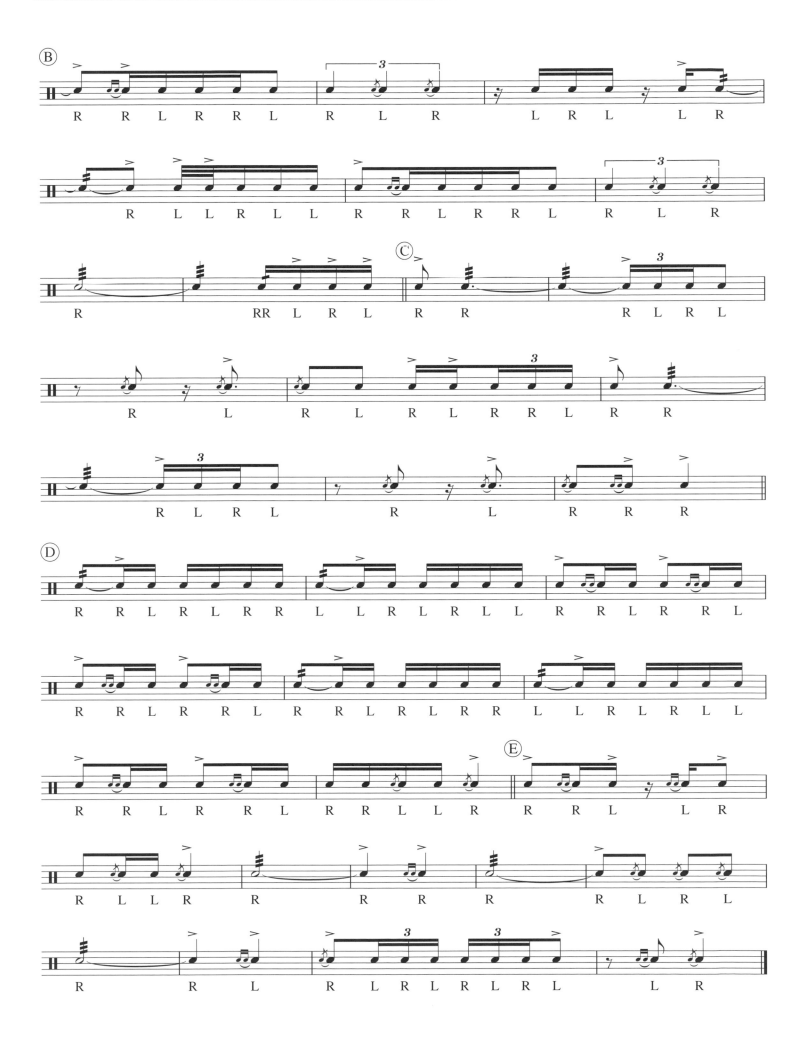

CHAPTER 33

Another Opportunity to Drum

CONCEPTS: This drumming opportunity includes rudimental stickings and 32nd notes.

READING: In this piece, you will find a variety of patterns and note denominations. Also find the challenge of reading stickings, which is an important part of the interpretation of this piece.

PHRASING: A powerful transition starts at measure 8 that utilizes a crescendo roll into *forte* 16th-note triplets.

The rhythms in measures 10 to 13 are somewhat "choppy," but this sets up the flowing 16th and 32nd note patterns to follow.

TECHNIQUE: Sticking variety, grace notes, rolls, and rapid single strokes all need to be carefully practiced to make this piece a success.

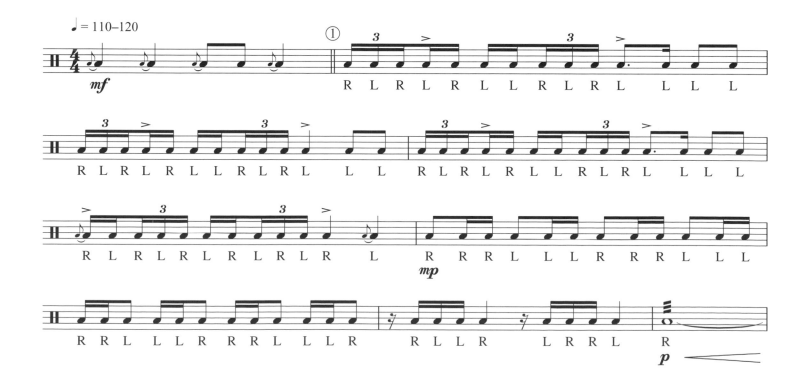

CHAPTER 34

Hold On a Minute

CONCEPT: "Hold On a Minute" presents changing tempos. It begins with a slow tempo with notated 32nd notes. A tempo modulation takes place at measures 21 to 22. The tempo will become faster, as the eighth note within the triplet becomes the natural eighth note of the meter.

READING: Quintuplets are introduced in measure 15. Quintuplets are an artificial grouping in which five 16th notes occur where normally we find four 16th notes. The spacing of the notes should be consistent.

Analyze the 32nd notes. Realize that the patterns are the same as many of the 16th-note patterns previously performed, but now they happen within half the time span. Using a metronome set on eighth notes will help with accuracy.

A21 to A22 is a tempo modulation. The individual 8th-note triplet notes will become the same speed as the 8th notes, therefore increasing the tempo of the pulse.

PHRASING: As always analyze how the phrases transition. At times, there is a connecting rhythm while at other times, the phrase may resolve, resulting in the next phrase starting unprepared. The above-mentioned tempo modulation is a good transitional effect, as a consistent pattern (flammed 8th notes) goes from being triplets to 8th notes.

TECHNIQUE: Tempo control is part of the technique with this piece.

Also, maintain stick control with the stickings and the dynamic changes.

CHAPTER 35

It's the Thought That Counts

CONCEPT: This piece utilizes three different thought processes. From A to B, the piece is to be performed exactly as notated. From B to C, you are to improvise, incorporating a variety of sounds and rhythms. You should be inspired by the music before and after the section to make it a completely musical translation. From C to D, perform exactly as notated. From D to E, perform the rhythms and incorporate your own interpretation of embellishments, which can include dynamics, stickings, articulations, various sound sources, and more.

READING: When reading the C section, perform it in such a way that it sounds natural to the preceding section.

The bass drum part under the buzz rolls at measures 20 and 21 is the lead voice. Perform it with more emphasis than the snare drum roll.

PHRASING: The thought process of each section changes, but try to make each phrase link in a musical way.

TECHNIQUE: Going from the open roll at E (bar 34) to the triplet roll (16th-note triplets) will require an immediate adjustment of stick control.

Open single stroke roll to closed roll in free time. The number of notes is arbitrary.

CHAPTER 36

Pinpoint It

CONCEPT: In "Pinpoint It," you will be splitting sporadic rhythms between the bass drum, hi-hats, and snare. You will experience mixed subdivisions going from triplets to sixteenth-note patterns. Watch accuracy and timing, as there is also rest usage, which can feel uncomfortable.

READING: Performing isolated attacks require careful thought of the note placement. Subdividing the groupings may be necessary. Allow the whole notes in the hi-hat part to ring.

PHRASING: Allow the notes to fall in place naturally and with relaxation. The rhythms are sporadic, but try to achieve a flowing sense of musical time.

TECHNIQUE: Technique should focus on coordination with the four limbs. Rhythmic accuracy, relaxation, and a good sense of touch will help provide the correct results.

CHAPTER 37

So Much More to Do

CONCEPT: "So Much More to Do" features flowing rudimental performance. Break down the patterns so that they feel natural and enjoyable to perform.

READING: When going from the 2/4 into the 12/8 at B , keep the pulse consistent.

PHRASING: The entire piece should have a consistent flow. Make the accents sing above the unaccented notes to draw attention to the rhythm they create.

TECHNIQUE: To be able to play a rudimental piece, you need to be able to have command over grace notes, rolls, and diddles. This piece is no exception.

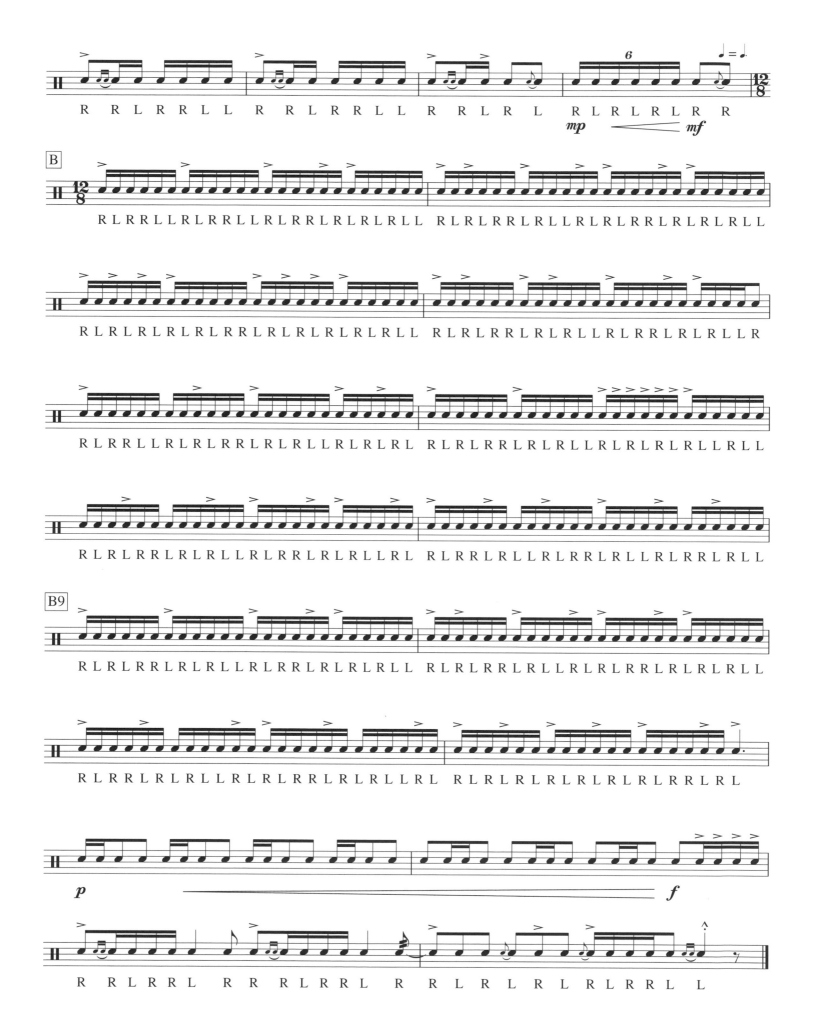

CHAPTER 38

On the Stage

CONCEPT: This piece is in 4/4 meter throughout with accents, rolls, flams, and more. Play it expressively, and it will get you *on the stage*!

READING: Syncopated accents and rhythms, plus triplets and rolls, make this piece an engaging experience.

PHRASING: The last beat of each phrase is as follows:

    sixteenth-note triplets with crescendo: bar 8

    sixteenth-note crescendo: bar 16

    sixteenth-note triplets into the drum rudiment called the *Lesson 25*:
        bar 21

    buzz roll ***fp*** crescendo: bar 27

TECHNIQUE: Within these sixteenth-note patterns, you encounter buzz rolls, open rolls, accents, flams, and more.

CHAPTER 39

Hit the Spot

CONCEPT: Changing meters and abrupt tempo changes.

READING: "Hit the Spot" includes reading with the snare drum and the bass drum. Observe the tempo markings.

In 6/8, you will find duplet groupings. These should divide the pulse precisely in half.

PHRASING: This piece starts with a 15-bar section.

At bar 16, after a fermata, a new tempo and a new time signature characterize an 11-bar phrase.

At bar 27, we suddenly enter a brisk tempo. A *D.S. al Coda* brings us back to the 6/8 for a dance-like ending.

TECHNIQUE: Observe your striking area, and do not allow your attention to the bass drum part distract you from maintaining a high quality snare drum tone.

CHAPTER 40

Focus!

CONCEPT: Mixed subdivisions, rudimental stickings, buzz rolls, changing meters, and more within a steady tempo throughout make this piece a captivating experience.

READING: Bar 1 starts with split up sixteenth-note triplets.

Measure 4 divides a quarter-note triplet into sixteenth notes. Break it down as needed.

Measure 24 to the end requires consistent playing motion. Allow it to flow.

PHRASING: Observe the rehearsal numbers as they define each phrase. Also, notice how the phrases are linked to each other.

At measure 46, we have a 5-note eighth-note pattern that repeats. The beaming displays this pattern. Notice how it affects the essence of the phrasing over the 4/4 time signature.

TECHNIQUE: When playing the paradiddles at measure 12, the rhythm of the sixteenth notes should be your first concern. The diddles will add an interesting articulation to your sound.

When playing the buzz rolls, observe the releases and individual notes. The attacks and releases are all part of the rhythmic phrasing. Also, strive for a smooth roll quality.

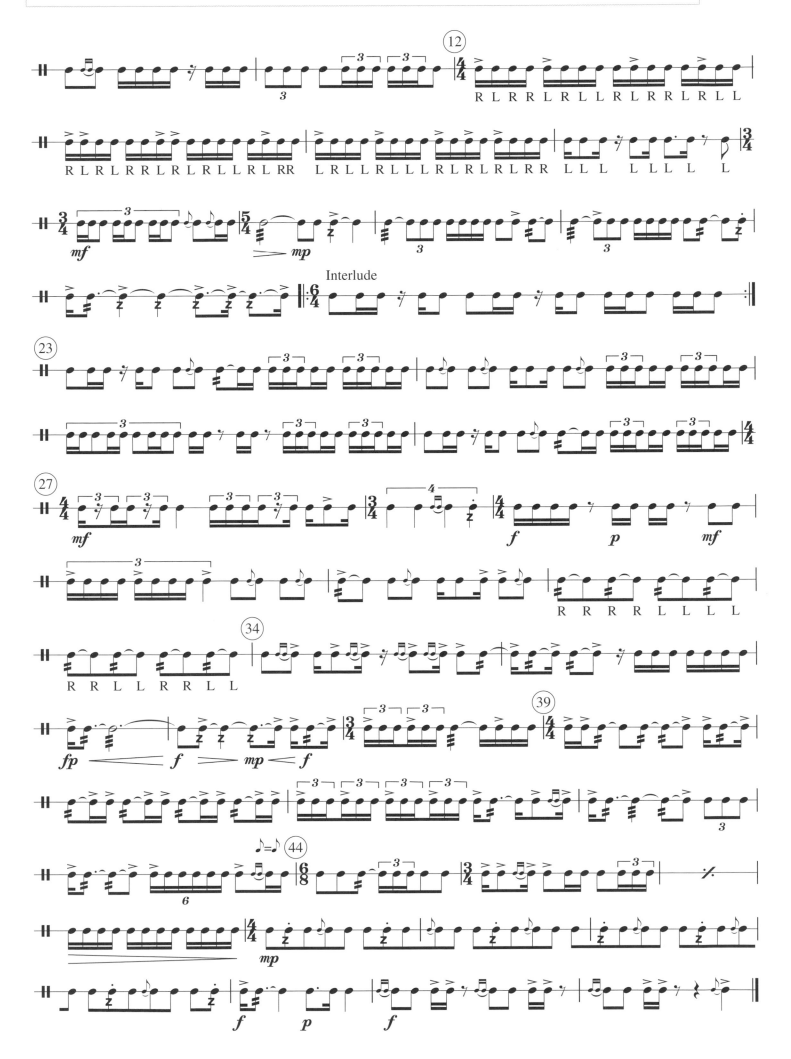

CHAPTER 41

Not So Random

CONCEPT: "Not So Random" features a fast tempo in 12/8 meter until measure 34.

PHRASING: Notice the abrupt tempo change on the fourth pulse of bar 34. There, the music starts a 3-pulse grouping over the 4-pulse of the 12/8.

READING: This piece is a fast 12/8 composition. The dotted-quarter note at 144 bpm goes into an immediate tempo change, with the dotted-quarter note becoming 76 bpm. Always try to look ahead.

TECHNIQUE: The notes inside the triplets that have one slash are to be played as double strokes. The result is the double-stroke roll. Because it is a precise rhythm, strive for rhythmic accuracy and a consistent articulation of the notes.

CHAPTER 42

Cracker Jacks and Daffodils

CONCEPT: "Cracker Jacks and Daffodils" includes a variety of sticking variations, special notations, and rhythmic variety.

READING: Amongst many sixteenth-note patterns, including sixteenth-note triplets, you move into a section with less activity at B9 with a three-pulse pattern phrased over 12/8. Be careful not to rush and watch the accuracy with the duplets. At B12 the hand parts will be similar to B9 to B11 but the pulse underneath will be faster.

PHRASING: Notice the beaming over the downbeats and the bar line beginning at A12. This method of beaming is used to display patterns that need to be expressed as individual units.

At measure 8, we have isolated attacks that divide the measure in half. Be careful of accuracy. Next, we have four sixteenths repeated but phrased over the downbeats and the bar line. Another measure occurs now in 4/4 and at the *mf* level to transition into a 12/8 section.

At B9, we begin another section with plenty of space. The pulse increases when you enter the 3/4 measure and continues to form a unique and resounding ending.

TECHNIQUE: Keep the rhythms accurate when performing them with stickings.

At B2, the first pulse includes a rhythm with stickings, the second pulse with a roll that divides the pulse in half, the third pulse that is syncopated and enhanced with double grace notes, and the fourth pulse with two accents, a pause, and a sixteenth-note triplet. A measure like this requires a high level of understanding and technique.

CHAPTER 43

A Great Time for All

CONCEPTS: "A Great Time for All" includes striking on the hi-hat cymbals.

READING: Reading here includes the snare drum, bass drum, and hi-hat cymbals with various tone explorations, meter changes, and stickings.

PHRASES: Maintain a constant flow through this piece as you vary the sound sources.

TECHNIQUE: This piece has movement from the snare drum to the hi-hat cymbals while needing to adjust to playing flams, rolls, accents, and more.

At measure 6, play the buzz rolls with the right hand only while the hi-hat cymbals will be struck with the left hand.

CHAPTER 44

Make It Groove

CONCEPT: The sixteenth notes with accents and buzz rolls should groove.

Notice the change of time signatures starting at measure thirteen, 6/4, 5/4, 4/4, 3/4, 2/4, and 1/4.

READING: The syncopated accents augment the rhythm. Accuracy is needed as any hesitation can throw the rhythm off, resulting in a complete loss of feel.

PHRASING: Notice the 6/4 measure at bar 13. The measure drops a beat going from 6/4 to 5/4 to 4/4 all the way to 1/4. This piece has several sections. Analyze it before playing it.

TECHNIQUE: Try to relax when playing the single-handed stickings, as the effect will be lost if your technique becomes stiff and forced.

CHAPTER 45

Emotional Connection

CONCEPT: Changing meters, syncopated rhythms, and a four-over-three transition will make "The Emotional Connection" close to your heart.

READING: Always keep the eighth note consistent when changing time signatures, unless otherwise indicated.

At times, 5/8 is grouped as 2 + 3, and at other times, it is grouped as 3 + 2.

PHRASING: The first section is twelve measures in 5/8 (2 + 3 grouping). The next 4-bar section has meter changes. The next 5-bar section ends with the four-over-three pattern. This pattern can feel like a tempo change. The next section (four bars in 4/4) is a transition that returns to 5/8. The last section incorporates some changing meters that lead up to a final measure in 1/4.

TECHNIQUE: Flams, ruffs, buzz rolls, and double-stroke rolls make up the technical repertoire of this piece. Carefully observe your sound quality as you play these embellishments, especially when changing meters.

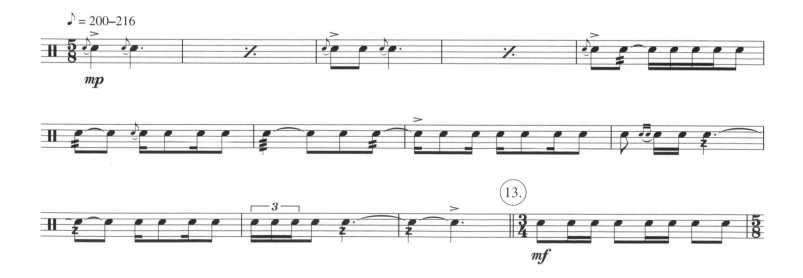

CHAPTER 46

A Different Angle

CONCEPTS: The emphasis is on changing meters. The eighth note is constant throughout.

READING: The 5/8 time signature starts with a 3 + 2 grouping.

   The grouping of notes in the 11/8 sections starting at bar 33 is unique. The 3 + 3 + 2 + 2 + 1 closes the gap between each pulsation. On the last eighth note, click the sticks together.

PHRASING: When the meters change frequently, there is a feeling of ongoing momentum. Let the natural pulsations of the measures lead you through the piece. The meters should create a dance-like effect that should be enjoyable to perform.

TECHNIQUE: Most rolls are to be played in an open manner in this piece. Be careful not to let the meter changes interfere with the high quality of tone you are striving for.

CHAPTER 47

Drumming Is Bliss

CONCEPT: This piece explores changing tempos. These tempo modulations require you to analyze how the designated note value will become a new value taking on a new role of importance. The change of value will force the tempo to either slow down or speed up. For example, the quarter-note triplets beginning in bar 6 will become the quarter notes in bar 9. This will increase the tempo.

READING: The rhythms used in this piece are quite common. Emphasis must be put into the tempo modulations. Analyze the modulations before attempting to play this piece.

PHRASING: Each new tempo will feel and sound like a new phrase. In this piece, the meters change at the tempo modulations, resulting in each section receiving its own character.

TECHNIQUE: There are not many intricate technical patterns here. The challenge is in the tempo changes and being expressive within each section. The 4-stroke ruff is in measure 1. This can be played with a variety of stickings:

CHAPTER 48

Provide the Elements

CONCEPT: "Provide the Elements" involves mixed meters, with the denominator alternating between 8 and 4.

READING: All of the measures with 8 as a denominator combine 2- and 3-note groupings. For example, the 15/8 is 3 + 3 + 3 + 2 + 2 + 2.

PHRASING: The frequent meter changes make this a rotating and revolving experience that will definitely require your focus. The 7/8 bar at measure 30 drives you into a long open 32nd note roll, to a triplet roll, to 16th notes with double sticking, to triplets with double stickings, to 8th notes with double stickings, and finally into quarter notes with double stickings accompanied with a decrescendo. A passage like this is exhilarating to listen to and to play, when performed correctly.

TECHNIQUE: The above-mentioned roll requires expert control of double strokes. Make sure that articulation is maintained with clear notes at each contact.

CHAPTER 49

Abrupt at Any Moment

CONCEPT: "Abrupt at Any Moment" highlights syncopated sixteenth-note triplets, which suddenly explode in the third measure of each 4-bar phrase in the first six lines and later in the composition.

READING: A large variety of rhythms exist here with scoring for the bass drum, hi-hats, and the snare drum.

PHRASING: After sixteen measures that include the exploding sixteenth-note triplets, there is an abrupt tempo change from 116 to 132 bpm. A long, accented buzz-roll pattern transitions into an open-sounding section with the bass drum and hi-hats carrying the lead. At bar 32, it returns to the original tempo, with the exploding accented triplets moving into a long roll, progressing with an accelerando to a fast and loud syncopated ending.

TECHNIQUE: It is best not to raise the sticks too high when playing the rapid sixteenth-note triplets, as the extra motion may slow you down.

Notice that you will be playing paradiddles with the feet starting on beat 2 of bar 29.

CHAPTER 50

7–9 Pump

CONCEPT: This piece has mixed meters with performance on the hi-hats, bass drum, and snare drum as the sound sources.

READING: Strike the hi-hat cymbals with one hand. Observe the groupings of the odd meters.

PHRASING: The 7/8 and 9/8 meters are phrased in two ways. First, phrase them as groupings of twos, with a 3-note pattern at the end. For example, the 7/8 is 2 + 2 + 3. Then in measure 15, it resembles a 4/4 measure but with one eighth note dropped. The same idea happens with the 9/8. At first, in measure 33, it is grouped as 2 + 2 + 2 + 3. Then at measure 41, it changes to resemble a 4/4 measure with one extra eighth note.

TECHNIQUE: When playing the eighth notes on the closed hi-hats, do not play the notes in a stiff and unexpressive manner. Instead, relax and provide a slight accent that goes along with the groupings.

About the Author

Shane Corcoran Photography LLC

Dave Vose, professor at Berklee College of Music, has been a percussion instructor, author, researcher, and clinician for many years. He has performed with such rock groups as the Drifters, Freddy Cannon, and Freedom. Dave is an artist clinician with the Zildjian Company, Grover Percussion, and the Yamaha Corporation of America. He has been a consultant, arranger, and teacher of many championship drum corps, including the North Star, Reading Buccaneers, Boston Crusaders, and the Cadets of Bergen County. He is also author of *The Reading Drummer* (Berklee Press, 2nd Edition 2006).

More Fine Publications from Berklee Press

GUITAR

BERKLEE BASIC GUITAR
by William Leavitt
Phase 1
50449460 Book Only $9.99
Phase 2
50449470 Book Only $9.95

BERKLEE BLUES GUITAR SONGBOOK
by Michael Williams
50449593 Book/CD Pack...................$24.99

**BERKLEE JAZZ GUITAR
CHORD DICTIONARY**
by Rick Peckham
50449546 Book $10.99

**BERKLEE ROCK GUITAR
CHORD DICTIONARY**
by Rick Peckham
50449596 Book $12.99

THE CHORD FACTORY
BUILD YOUR OWN GUITAR CHORD
DICTIONARY
by Jon Damian
50449541 Book $24.95

FUNK/R&B GUITAR
by Thaddeus Hogarth
50449569 Book/CD.............................$19.95

JAZZ IMPROVISATION FOR GUITAR
by Garrison Fewell
A Harmonic Approach
50449594 Book/CD Pack......................$24.99
A Melodic Approach
50449503 Book/CD Pack......................$24.99

A MODERN METHOD FOR GUITAR
by William Leavitt
Volume 1: Beginner
50449404 Book/CD.............................$22.95
50449400 Book Only $14.95
50448066 DVD...................................$29.95
50448065 Book/DVD-ROM $34.99
Volume 2: Intermediate
50449410 Book Only $14.95
Volume 3: Advanced
50449420 Book $16.95
Jazz Songbook, Vol. 1
50449539 Book/CD $14.99
123 Complete
by William Leavitt
50449468 Book $34.95

MELODIC RHYTHMS FOR GUITAR
by William Leavitt
50449450 Book $14.95

PLAYING THE CHANGES: GUITAR
by Mitch Seidman and Paul Del Nero
50449509 Book/CD Pack......................$19.95

BASS

**CHORD STUDIES FOR
ELECTRIC BASS**
by Rich Appleman
50449750 Book $16.99

FINGERSTYLE FUNK BASS LINES
by Joe Santerre
50449542 Book/CD Pack......................$19.95

INSTANT BASS
by Danny Morris
50449502 Book/CD.............................$14.95

**READING CONTEMPORARY
ELECTRIC BASS**
by Rich Appleman
50449770 Book $19.95

ROCK BASS LINES
by Joe Santerre
50449478 Book/CD.............................$19.95

Berklee Press Publications feature material
developed at the Berklee College of Music.

To browse the Berklee Press Catalog, go to
www.berkleepress.com

DRUM SET AND PERCUSSION

**CREATIVE JAZZ IMPROVISATION
FOR DRUM SET**
by Yoron Israel
50449549 DVD....................................$24.95

DRUM SET WARM-UPS
by Rod Morgenstein
50449465 Book $12.95

EIGHT ESSENTIALS OF DRUMMING
by Ron Savage
50448048 Book/CD $19.99

NEW WORLD DRUMMING
by Pablo Peña "Pablitodrum"
50449547 DVD....................................$24.95

**TURNTABLE TECHNIQUE:
THE ART OF THE DJ - 2ND EDITION**
by Stephen Webber
50449482 Book/2-Record Set $34.99

OTHER INSTRUMENTS

BLUEGRASS FIDDLE AND BEYOND
by Matt Glaser
50449602 Book/CD Pack...................$19.99

BLUEGRASS BANJO AND BEYOND
by Matt Glaser
50449610 Book/CD Pack...................$19.99

BEYOND BLUEGRASS MANDOLIN
by Matt Glaser and John McGann
50449609 Book/CD Pack...................$19.99

IMPROVISATION FOR FLUTE
by Andy McGhee
50449810 Book $14.99

IMPROVISATION FOR SAXOPHONE
by Andy McGhee
50449860 Book $14.99

VOICE

**THE CONTEMPORARY SINGER –
2ND EDITION**
by Anne Peckham
50449595 Book/CD.............................$24.99

**VOCAL WORKOUTS FOR THE
CONTEMPORARY SINGER**
by Anne Peckham
50448044 Book/CD.............................$24.95

SINGER'S HANDBOOK
by Anne Peckham
50448053 Book $9.95

TIPS FOR SINGERS
by Carolyn Wilkins
50449557 Book/CD Pack...................$19.95

BERKLEE PRACTICE METHOD

with additional volumes for six other instruments, plus a teacher's guide

GUITAR
by Larry Baione
50449426 Book/CD $14.95

KEYBOARD
by Paul Schmeling and Russell Hoffmann
50449428 Book/CD $14.95

BASS
by Rich Appleman and John Repucci
50449427 Book/CD $14.95

DRUM SET
by Casey Scheuerell and Ron Savage
50449429 Book/CD $14.95

KEYBOARD

BERKLEE JAZZ PIANO
by Ray Santisi
50448047 Book/CD $19.99

HAMMOND ORGAN COMPLETE
by Dave Limina
50449479 Book/CD $24.95

PIANO ESSENTIALS
by Ross Ramsay
50448046 Book/CD $24.95

SOLO JAZZ PIANO
by Neil Olmstead
50449444 Book/CD $39.95

IMPROVISATION SERIES

BLUES IMPROVISATION COMPLETE
by Jeff Harrington
50449486 B♭ Instruments......................$19.95
50449488 C Bass Instruments $19.95
50449425 C Treble Instruments $22.99
50449487 E♭ Instruments......................$19.95

A GUIDE TO JAZZ IMPROVISATION
by John LaPorta
50449439 C Instruments $19.95
50449441 B♭ Instruments.................$19.99
50449442 E♭ Instruments.................$19.99
50449443 Bass Clef $19.99

GENERAL MUSIC

BEGINNING EAR TRAINING
by Gilson Schachnik
50449548 Book/CD $14.95

BERKLEE MUSIC THEORY
by Paul Schmeling
Book 1
50448043 Book/CD $24.95
Book 2
50448062 Book/CD $22.95

ESSENTIAL EAR TRAINING
by Steve Prosser
50449421 Book $16.95

MUSIC NOTATION
by Mark McGrain
50449399 Book $24.95

MUSIC NOTATION
Preparing Scores and Parts
by Matthew Nicholl and Richard Grudzinski
50449540 Book $16.95

MUSIC SMARTS
by Mr. Bonzai
edited by David Schwartz
50449591 Book $14.99

MUSICIAN'S YOGA
by Mia Olson
50449587 Book $14.99

THE NEW MUSIC THERAPIST'S HANDBOOK, SECOND EDITION
by Suzanne B. Hanser
50449424 Book $29.95

MUSIC BUSINESS

THE FUTURE OF MUSIC
by Dave Kusek & Gerd Leonhard
50448055 Book $16.95

HOW TO GET A JOB IN THE MUSIC INDUSTRY – 2ND EDITION
by Keith Hatschek
50449551 Book $27.95

MAKING MUSIC MAKE MONEY
by Eric Beall
50448009 Book $26.95

MUSIC LAW IN THE DIGITAL AGE
by Allen Bargfrede and Cecily Mak
50449586 Book $19.99

MUSIC MARKETING
by Mike King
50449588 Book $24.99

THE SELF-PROMOTING MUSICIAN – 2ND EDITION
by Peter Spellman
50449589 Book $24.95

MUSIC PRODUCTION & ENGINEERING

MIX MASTERS
by Maureen Droney
50448023 Book $24.95

PRODUCING IN THE HOME STUDIO WITH PRO TOOLS – 3RD EDITION
by David Franz
50449544 Book/DVD-ROM $39.95

PRODUCING & MIXING CONTEMPORARY JAZZ
by Dan Moretti
50449554 Book/DVD-ROM $24.95

PRODUCING AND MIXING HIP-HOP/R&B
by Mike Hamilton
50449555 Book/DVD-ROM Pack $19.99

PRODUCING DRUM BEATS
by Eric Hawkins
50449598 Book/CD-ROM Pack......................$22.99

UNDERSTANDING AUDIO
by Daniel M. Thompson
50449456 Book $24.99

SONGWRITING, COMPOSING, ARRANGING

COMPLETE GUIDE TO FILM SCORING – 2ND EDITION
by Richard Davis
50449607 Book $27.99

JAZZ COMPOSITION
by Ted Pease
50448000 Book/CD Pack $39.99

MELODY IN SONGWRITING
by Jack Perricone
50449419 Book $24.95

MODERN JAZZ VOICINGS
by Ted Pease and Ken Pullig
50449485 Book/CD $24.95

MUSIC NOTATION
by Mark McGrain
50449399 Book $24.95

MUSIC NOTATION
Preparing Scores and Parts
by Matthew Nicholl and Richard Grudzinski
50449540 Book $16.95

POPULAR LYRIC WRITING
by Andrea Stolpe
50449553 Book $14.95

THE SONGWRITER'S WORKSHOP: HARMONY
by Jimmy Kachulis
50449519 Book/CD $29.95

THE SONGWRITER'S WORKSHOP: MELODY
by Jimmy Kachulis
50449518 Book/CD Pack $24.95

SONGWRITING: ESSENTIAL GUIDE TO LYRIC FORM AND STRUCTURE
by Pat Pattison
50481582 Book $16.95

SONGWRITING: ESSENTIAL GUIDE TO RHYMING
by Pat Pattison
50481583 Book $14.95

FOR MORE INFORMATION,
SEE YOUR LOCAL MUSIC DEALER,
OR WRITE TO:

HAL•LEONARD®
CORPORATION
7777 W. BLUEMOUND RD. P.O. BOX 13819
MILWAUKEE, WISCONSIN 53213

Prices subject to change without notice. Visit your local music dealer or bookstore, or go to **www.berkleepress.com**